cello

⊕ making jazz easy in the string orchestra

JAZZ

philharmonic

randy **sabien** & bob phillips

Alfred Publishing Co., Inc.
16320 Roscoe Blvd., Suite 100
P.O. Box 10003
Van Nuys, CA 91410-0003
alfred.com

19594 (Book) ISBN-10: 0-7390-1040-9
ISBN-13: 978-0-7390-1040-2

26303 (Book/CD) ISBN-10: 0-7390-4416-8
ISBN-13: 978-0-7390-4416-2

Copyright © 2000 by Alfred Publishing Co., Inc.
All rights reserved. Printed in USA.

MW00594215

randy sabien

As a fourth grader in Rockford, IL, Randy dreamed of playing drums in a rock and roll band. At the same time, his drum and orchestra teacher, Don Zimmerman, dreamed of building up the string section in the school orchestra, so Randy soon found himself studying violin with Hannah Armstrong—a relationship that would last until he left for college in 1974. Afterward, at the University of Illinois, the world of etudes, concertos and symphonies merged with the world of pop music, garage bands and electric guitars through the medium of improvised jazz.

A leader of his own jazz groups nationwide since 1983, Randy has played folk music with Rock and Roll Hall of Fame inductees Jim Post, Mimi Farina, Kate Wolf and Greg Brown, and has appeared on the *Prairie Home Companion* radio show and PBS's *Austin City Limits*. To his credit are several critically acclaimed recordings on his own label. A pioneer in jazz education, he founded the string department at the Berklee College of Music in 1978, and he has conducted jazz clinics for thousands of string students and teachers, including the International String Workshops in Europe. Randy currently resides in Hayward, WI. To contact him about performances, workshops or recordings, check out his web site at www.randysabien.com.

bob phillips

Director of public school orchestras in Saline, MI, Bob is nationally renowned as a string educator and innovator in string education, co-authoring the popular folk fiddling series *Fiddlers Philharmonic* and *Fiddlers Philharmonic Encore!*, published by Alfred Publishing Company. Bob is also founder of the high school folk fiddling ensemble, Fiddlers Philharmonic. Under his direction, the Fiddlers have performed in settings from bluegrass festivals to the White House and have released three recordings. To learn more, visit their web site at www.salinefiddlers.com.

Bob received his B.M. and M.M. from the University of Michigan, studying double bass with Lawrence Hurst and music education with Elizabeth Green, Robert Culver and James Froseth. He has been recognized as teacher of the year by various professional music organizations. He has been invited to present clinics in twenty states and seven countries including the MENC/ASTA National Convention, the International String Workshops, the Mid-West International Band and Orchestra Clinic and the International Society of Bassists Convention. He has conducted many youth orchestras and camps.

Special thanks to our friends and mentors, Marvin Rabin, Jerry Fishbach and Bob Culver.

table of contents

introduction

When Randy Sabien was a music student, he accidentally discovered a recording by the great jazz violinist, Stephane Grappelli. A whole new world opened for him and he realized immediately that he wanted to play jazz on the violin and also share this newfound world with young string players everywhere. The first tune Randy attempted to learn on his own was John Coltrane's "Giant Steps," one of the most difficult jazz tunes ever written. Although frustrated by the complexity of Coltrane's masterpiece, Randy eventually learned to play jazz through an old fashioned system called trial and error. After 25 years as an internationally renowned jazz artist, Randy teamed up with Bob Phillips, an educator well known for his innovative use of alternative music in the string curriculum. The result is *Jazz Philharmonic*, a pedagogically sequenced book of original jazz tunes that allows students to begin a journey into the world of jazz and other popular styles of music.

The layout of the book includes a Preparatory Page for each tune. Echo back each phrase Randy plays on the CD to develop a sense of jazz style and timing. Mastery of the Preparatory Page building blocks will prepare you to play the tunes, add solos and begin improvising. The Tune and Background Page includes background parts for the violins and violas while the cellos and basses also learn to play jazz bass lines. The Solos Page introduces two progressively difficult jazz solos based on the tune. Developing arrangements is easy; some students can play the tune while others play a background or bass part. Individuals or sections can take turns playing the written-out solos as well as improvising new solos. Easy piano parts are included in the teacher's manual so a complete rhythm section can be added to the strings. If no rhythm section is available, the CD can be used in performance. The left channel features Randy performing all the written tunes and solos and several choruses of improvisation. The right channel features a professional rhythm section playing all the Background 2 and Bass 2 parts. By panning right or left you can play along with Randy or the rhythm section. The CD creates a great avenue for beginning improvisation as well as playing some great jazz tunes.

Put on the CD, learn the tunes and play along with Randy and the band.

P.S. It's 25 years later and Randy still can't play "Giant Steps," but maybe you will.

groovin' for the first time tune and background

track **three**

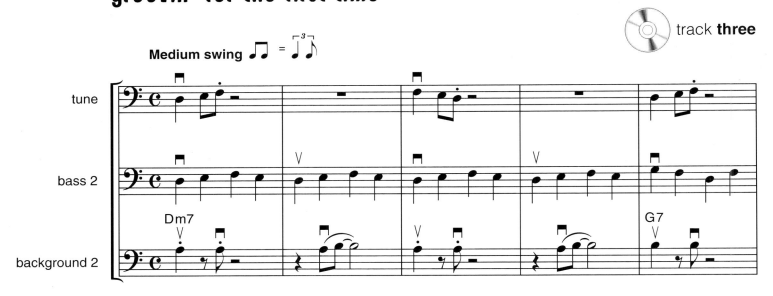

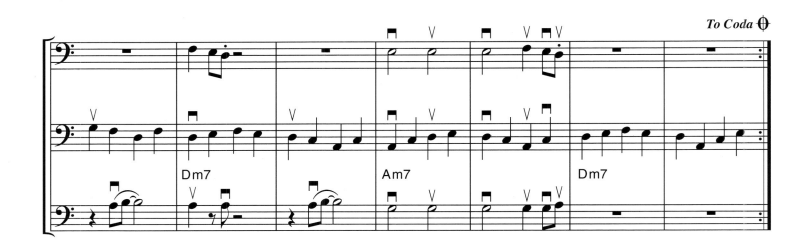

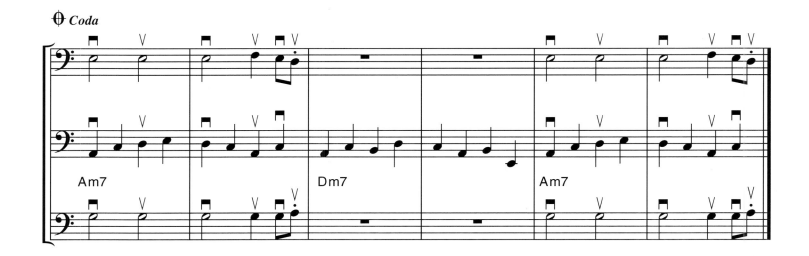

Preparatory Page—see page 6.

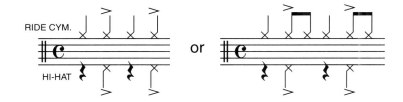

groovin' for the first time **solos**

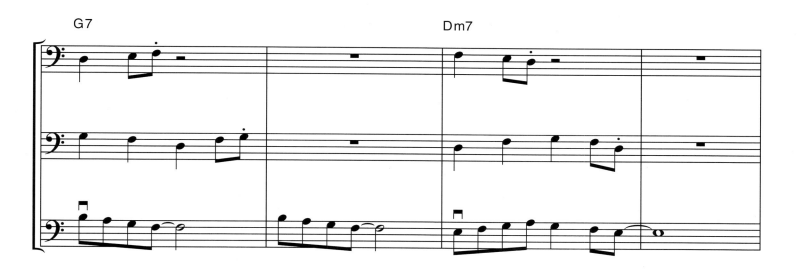

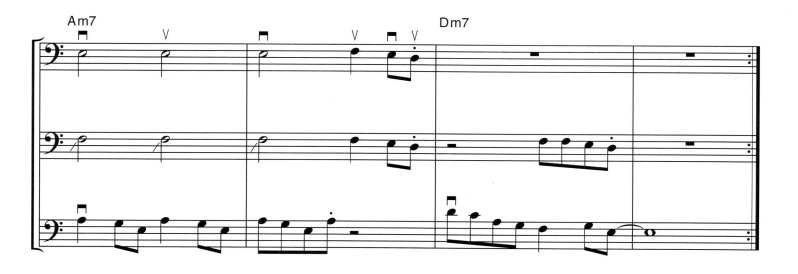

groovin' for the first time preparatory page

This three-note melody uses lots of space between each phrase. "Groovin' for the First Time" captures the essence of swinging jazz at a laid back tempo. Swing involves playing eighth notes in an uneven manner, which you will hear in Randys playing. Miles Davis captured this mood of rhythmic momentum on his album *Kind of Blue,* which should be the first jazz recording you purchase.

track **two**

D Dorian Scale (C scale starting on D)

One-Bar Rhythmic Echoes

Two-Bar Rhythmic Echoes

One-Bar Melodic Echoes

Two-Bar Melodic Echoes

de blues preparatory page

"De Blues" is another example of a melody using only a few notes with lots of space between phrases. A musical form native to the U.S., blues is the funky, earthy, rolling style which began as a three-line chant, resulting in 12 bars, or three lines of four. Blues uses the idea of "bent" pitch, imitating a voice sliding between pitches. The background rhythm has a hard driving beat called a shuffle. Check out Kansas City pianist Jay McShann and violinist Claude Williams.

track **four**

de blues tune and background

track **five**

de blues solos

daydream preparatory page

When you're learning something new, it's a good idea to play it slowly. A ballad like "Daydream" is supposed to be played slowly, so relax and let this tune float beautifully out of your instrument. Listen to "Mood Indigo" or "In a Sentimental Mood" by Duke Ellington.

track **six**

G Major Scale

One-Bar Rhythmic Echoes

Two-Bar Rhythmic Echoes

One-Bar Melodic Echoes

Two-Bar Melodic Echoes

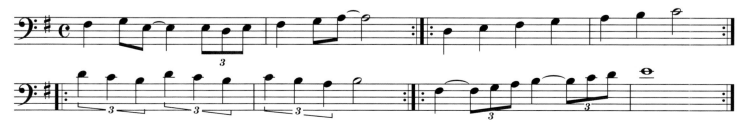

daydream tune and backgrounds

track seven

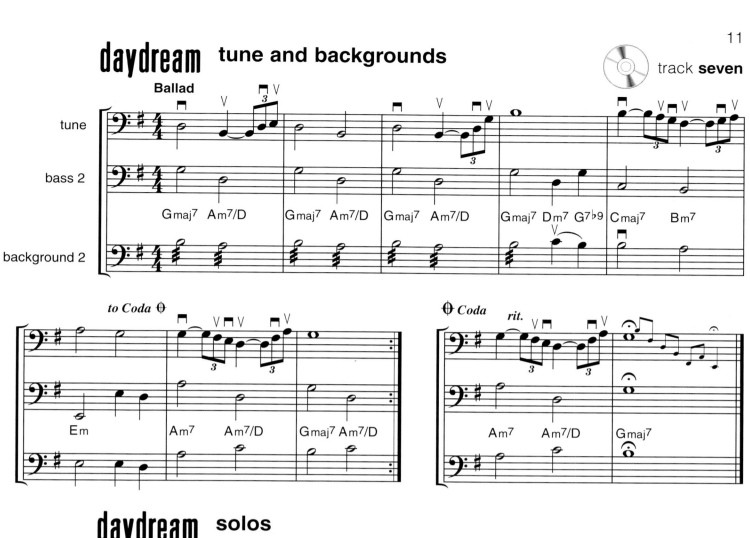

daydream solos

devious tune and background

track **nine**

Preparatory Page—see page 14.

devious solos

devious preparatory page

"Devious" uses straight or even eighth notes like the eighth notes in classical music. There are many different kinds of Latin rhythms and most jazz musicians incorporate this style into their repertoire. Listen to Duke Ellington's "Caravan" and Dizzy Gillespie's "A Night in Tunisia". Both of these tunes alternate between a "straight" feel and a "swing" feel. *Devious* is played straight all the way.

track **eight**

shout it out preparatory page

They say jazz was created in New Orleans, but there's a lot more down there than ragtime and Dixieland. It's a huge gumbo of blues, gospel, funk, Cajun, soul, country, Caribbean and other influences. The jazz of "Shout It Out" is gospel rock. Listen to Dr. John, Professor Longhair, Irma Thomas, and the Neville Brothers for starters.

track **ten**

shout it out tune and background

track **eleven**

shout it out solos

latin doll tune and background

track **thirteen**

Preparatory Page—see page 20.

latin doll **solos**

latin doll preparatory page

Superimpose a blues scale over a Latin groove (straight eighths) with a backbeat, and you have a style of Latin-rock perfected by guitarist Carlos Santana. Remember a blues scale contains a lowered third, fifth and seventh.

track **twelve**

fiddle funk **preparatory page**

Funk is a specialized style of blues and rock perfected in the 1960s by James Brown with the help of drummer Clyde Stubblefield. It is played with straight eighth notes. Listen to anything by James Brown or to John Scofield's album *A Go Go.* The rhythmic patterns invented by Clyde Stubblefield are the basis for most of the contemporary hip hop and rap tunes of the 1990s and are illustrated in "Fiddle Funk."

track **fourteen**

fiddle funk tune and background

track **fifteen**

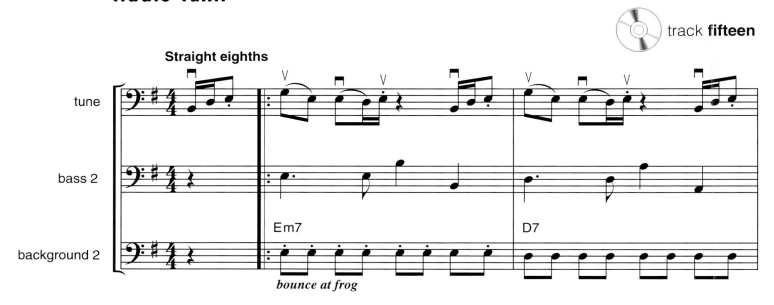

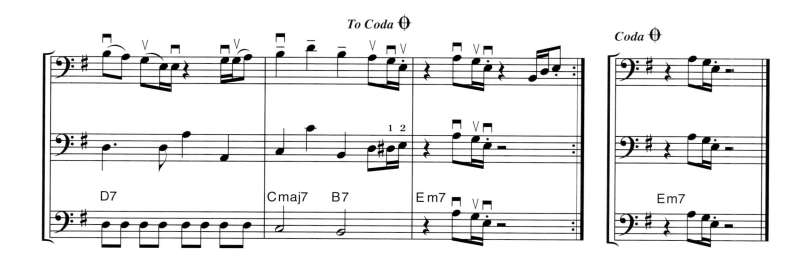

fiddle funk solos

tune
solo 1
solo 2

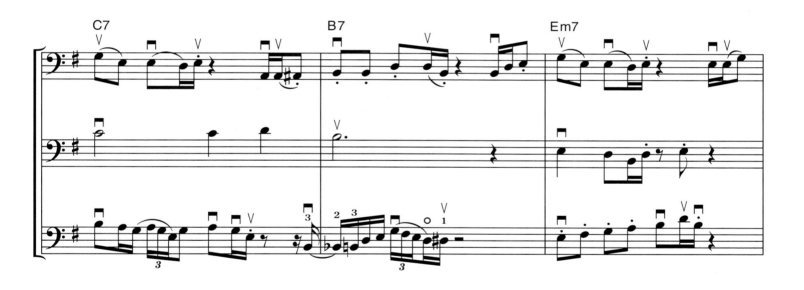

janie be good tune and background

track **seventeen**

Chuck Berry-style rock
Straight eighths

Preparatory Page—see page 26.

janie be good solos

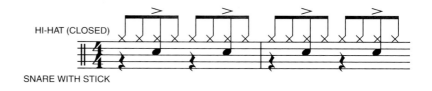

janie be good **preparatory page**

If you straighten out the eighth notes on "De Blues" or "Bop around the Clock" you would have good old-fashioned rock and roll like "Janie Be Good." Go to the source and listen to Chuck Berry. Don't overlook his piano player Johnny Johnson who also has some excellent recordings.

track **sixteen**

deep blue sea preparatory page

Here is a slow blues tune based on guitar styles made famous by T. Bone Walker and Muddy Waters. Fretless stringed instruments are perfect for this because you can slide your fingers in and out of the notes like a guitarist bending the pitches, to create a very soulful, emotional sound like that of the "Deep Blue Sea."

track **eighteen**

deep blue sea tune and background

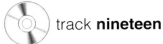
track **nineteen**

deep blue sea solos

in the mode
tune and background

track **twenty-one**

tune

bass 2

background 2

Preparatory Page—see page 32.

in the mode solos

in the mode preparatory page

"In the Mode" has two sections. The first half is played over the rhythm section, hitting only on 2 and 4. The walking bass line and the steady beat on the ride cymbal identify the second section. By listening to these two different parts, you can keep track of where you are in the piece. This introduces more complex forms. A group known for surprises is Art Blakey and the Jazz Messengers.

track **twenty**

bop around the clock preparatory page

"Bop around the Clock" with its up-tempo swinging groove and solid backbeat on 2 and 4 shows how rock and roll grew out of jazz. Listen to anything by Louis Jordan or to Duke Ellington's historic album *Live at Newport* (particularly "Diminuendo and Crescendo in Blue") then jump to Elvis Presley's "Don't Be Cruel" and Bill Haley's" Rock around the Clock." Early rock and roll was swing music!

track **twenty-two**

bop around the clock tune and background

track **twenty-three**

bop around the clock solos

sundance tune and background

track **twenty-five**

Preparatory Page—see page 40.

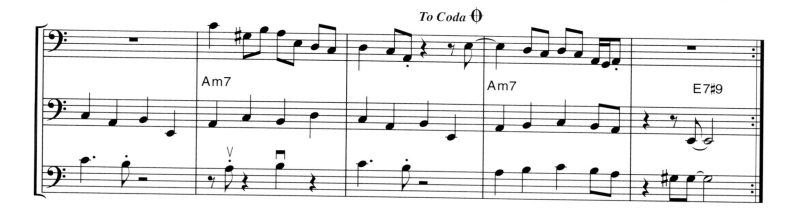

sundance solos

sundance **preparatory page**

Jazz has influenced popular singer/songwriters such as Van Morrison. His huge hit "Moondance" has a swinging rhythm with a walking bass line. "Sundance" introduces the longest form you'll encounter in this book—32 measures consisting of two 8-bar sections that are similar (the A sections) then an 8-bar section with new material (called the bridge or B section), then back to an 8-bar section like the beginning (A section). Put it all together and you have a form that looks like this: AABA. See if you can keep track of the different sections as you play. The rhythm section will be giving you clues!

track **twenty-four**